SACRAMENTO PUBLIC LIBRARY
828 "I" Street
Sacramento, CA 95814
12/20

D0572346

COPYCAT SCIENCE

Written and illustrated by
Mike Barfield

WITHDRAWN FROM COLLECTION
OF SACRAMENTO PUBLIC LIBRARY

CONTENTS

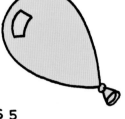

For science teachers everywhere,
especially Professor Patricia Wiltshire,
a true original—M.B.

Quarto is the authority on a wide range of topics.
Quarto educates, entertains and enriches the lives of
our readers—enthusiasts and lovers of hands-on living.
www.quartoknows.com

Consultant: Professor Charlotte Sleigh
Designer: Kevin Knight
Editor: Harriet Stone
Art Director: Susi Martin
Creative Director: Malena Stojic
Group Publisher: Maxime Boucknooghe

© 2020 Quarto Publishing plc
Text and Illustration © 2020 Mike Barfield

First published in 2020 by QED Publishing,
an imprint of The Quarto Group.
26391 Crown Valley Parkway, Suite 220
Mission Viejo, CA 92691, USA
T: +1 949 380 7510
F: +1 949 380 7575
www.QuartoKnows.com

All rights reserved. No part of this publication may
be reproduced, stored in a retrieval system, or
transmitted in any form or by any means,
electronic, mechanical, photocopying, recording, or
otherwise, without the prior permission of the
publisher, nor be otherwise circulated in any form
of binding or cover other than that in which it is
published and without a similar condition being
imposed on the subsequent purchaser.

A CIP record for this book is available from the
Library of Congress.

ISBN: 978-0-7112-5182-3

Printed in Guangdong, China TT062020

9 8 7 6 5 4 3 2 1

MIX
Paper from
responsible sources
FSC® C016973
www.fsc.org

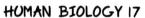

Hello, and welcome to "Copycat Science!"

I'm the funny-looking guy on the cover.

See page 70

But, this book is NOT about me!

It's NOT about any of these clever people either.

It isn't? What? Eh? No? Really? Aw, shucks!

This book is actually about YOU!

First, YOU read about these people's amazing lives...

ELECTRICITY   MATH   LIGHT   INSECTS   SPACE
COMETS

Then YOU copy some of their experiments.

Great!

ALL good scientists learn from the work of those before them.

That's true!

So, get reading and get copying!

Copy that!

Scientists build on the work of others. Begin your super science journey now!

LIVING THINGS

Learn about plants and animals
with these living experiments.

MARIA SIBYLLA MERIAN
"INSECT INSPECTOR"

BORN:
1647, Germany
DIED:
1717, The Netherlands

Maria Merian was a pioneering wildlife artist.

I was one of the first to study insects closely.

BZZZ!

Some of the insects studied her closely too!

Buzz off!

Maria's interest in insects started early.

I'm only young.

Me too.

← MINI-MARIA

Maria collected caterpillars from the countryside.

At the age of 13, she raised silkworms at home.

Yuk! Worms!

They're not worms, they're insects!

Silkworms are actually the larvae (caterpillars) of the silkworm moth.

Trained as an artist by her stepfather, Maria recorded every stage in their lifecycle.

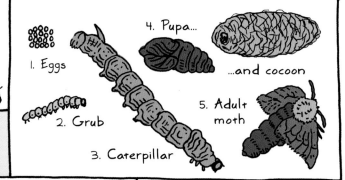

1. Eggs
2. Grub
3. Caterpillar
4. Pupa...
...and cocoon
5. Adult moth

Maria saw that caterpillars hatched from eggs.

That's right, we do!

Previously, many scientists thought caterpillars sprang magically from mud...

A crazy idea known as "spontaneous generation."

But, as I showed, good science is all about experimenting, observing, and recording...

And you're never too young to start.

True!

Maria was a brilliant insect scientist (entomologist). Now start some insect science yourself!

☆ Amazingly, nine out of ten animals on the planet is an insect! They dominate the land, and you can find them everywhere—including in your yard!

☆ Not all "creepy-crawlies" are insects. Most adult insects have six legs, a hard outside skeleton, and a body in three parts. Many also have wings, though they may be hidden away.

FOREWING
HEAD
THORAX
HINDWING
ABDOMEN
MOTH

~ My wings are hidden away!
LADYBUG

FLY   ANT   APHID

These are all types of insects.

SLUG   SPIDER   WOODLOUSE   CENTIPEDE

These are <u>not</u> insects.

BACKYARD SAFARI

You will need:

BOX   WHITE PAPER

MAGNIFYING GLASS

1 Line the bottom of a cardboard box with white paper.

2 Place the box under a bush or tree and shake the branches gently.

3 Count the legs of any animals that fall into the box. How many are insects?

✓ Release your specimens when you have finished.

THEOPHRASTUS
"ANCIENT GREEK LEAF GEEK"

BORN:
about 371 BCE, Greece
DIED:
about 287 BCE, Greece

Theophrastus was a Greek scientist born over 2,000 years ago.

Looking good for my age!

Modern scientists call him "the father of botany."

Hi, dad!

Botany is the science of plants.

His teacher was the great thinker Aristotle, who didn't rate plants at all.

ARISTOTLE

What a weed!

How rude!

But teachers aren't always right! We now know plants are vital for life on Earth.

Ha!

My bad...

Plants provide habitats, food, and the oxygen we need to breathe.

Theophrastus, however, loved plants —especially the ones he could eat!

I'm not snacking... it's research.

CHOMP!

He set out to describe all the different types.

I think this one's a creeper!

STRUGGLE!

We now think there are about 400,000 plant species.

Theophrastus also studied how plants reproduced.

Some by seeds, some by roots...

And some by both, like me!

He then wrote up everything he knew in two amazing books.

Don't worry, you're in them.

Fame!

But sadly they went missing for centuries.

All that work, LOST!

Shame!

Luckily, Theo's works surfaced again in the Middle Ages. Now try your own plant experiment.

UP-SEED-DOWN

 Theophrastus was very interested in how seeds germinated. With this simple experiment, you can see for yourself!

You will need:

BROAD BEAN SEEDS

CLEAN GLASS JAR

CARDSTOCK

PEN

PAPER TOWELS

1 Line the inside of the jar with a tube of folded and rolled paper towels, several layers thick.

2 Roll the cardstock into a tube and slip it inside the paper towels tube.

 The cardstock helps keep the paper towels against the glass.

3  Now examine your broad bean seeds. Look for this pointy little bump.

4 Choose two seeds and mark an arrow on each, pointing toward the end with the bump.

5 Tuck them down the sides of the jar—one pointing up, the other pointing down.

6 Add water inside the jar. Make sure the paper towels are always kept damp.

7 After a few days, the beans should begin to germinate—starting with a simple root called a radicle, and then growing a stalk upward.

 RADICLE

8 Eventually you will get a small bean seedling that you can replant in soil.

But what happens with the bean seed that was planted the other way up?

 Try the experiment and find out!

NEHEMIAH GREW AND STEPHEN HALES
"PIONEERING PLANT PEOPLE"

This is Nehemiah Grew.

Hi there!

BORN: England, 1641
DIED: England, 1712

This is Stephen Hales.

That's me!

BORN: England, 1677
DIED: England, 1761

And both of them are wearing wigs...

Why is yours so small?

Why is yours so big?

They also share a passion for plant anatomy.

No one had been as passionate since Theophrastus!

True!

Grew looked inside plants using the newly invented microscope and drew what he saw.

I, Grew, drew cells!

MICROSCOPE

ARTICHOKE CELLS

Grew saw that plants had different cell types.

While Hales did experiments to see how water moves inside plants.

The only way was up!

Yes, Hales here found that water travels from the roots to the leaves, then out into the air.

It's called "transpiration."

Any questions?

Why is your wig so big?

With or without a wig, why not investigate transpiration in plants yourself?

CUT AND DYED

 Hales and Grew increased our understanding of what happens inside plants.

 People used to think that plant sap circulated like the blood in humans. Wrong!

 This colorful experiment will reveal some of the secrets of transpiration!

You will need:

 SOME STURDY JARS OR GLASSES

 FOOD DYES IN STRONG COLORS

 FRESH CELERY STEMS (with or without leaves)

LETTUCE LEAVES

---

1 Half fill the glasses or jars with cold water and add some food coloring to each one.

☑ Red and blue work well.

2 Ask a grown-up to help cut off the last inch (2.5 cm) of the celery and lettuce using a kitchen knife.

CUT!

CUT!

---

3 Immediately place the plants into the dyed water so that the cut surfaces are under the water.

Don't knock me over!

4 *We're so pretty!* After about half an hour you should see the dye spreading up inside the plant tissues.

---

5 Dye may even travel as far as the leaf tips! This shows that water moves upward in plants, from the roots, to the stems, to the leaves, and then out into the air.

6 Cut across your specimens to reveal the bundles of tissues (xylem) that transported the dyed water!

CELERY

LETTUCE

CHARLES DARWIN
"EARTHWORM EXPERT"

BORN:
1809, England
DIED:
1882, England

Hello. I'm Charles Darwin, and I'm very old.

FLUTTER!

Darwin in 1881

People remember me best for my Theory of Evolution (how new species develop).

GALAPAGOS FINCHES

But my very last book was about something different. Something far more "down to earth"...

...worms!

Hello!

Hi!

Yo!

Through his research Darwin realized that worms are wonderful creatures!

CLITELLUM ("SADDLE")   SEGMENTS   ANUS

MOUTH

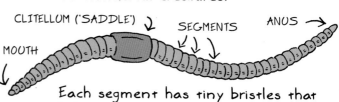

Each segment has tiny bristles that help worms move through the soil.

Worms are both male and female (hermaphrodite) and can neither hear nor see, yet they turn away from light!

TOOT-TOOT!

Sorry, nothing...

I proved they were deaf by asking my son to play the bassoon to them.

Most importantly, I saw how hard they work. Their burrows break up the soil and their poop keeps it full of nutrients. We owe worms a big thank you!

Just doing our thing!

CHOMP!

Now watch the wonders of worms for yourself by making an upcycled wormery!

WORM-WORLD

⭐ Darwin was wowed by how worms turned over the soil by pulling down dead plant matter, then bringing their poop (wormcasts) and fresh soil back to the surface.

✓ Make this recyclable "worm-world" to watch worms in action!

You will need:

CLEAN 2 LITER SODA BOTTLE

ALUMINUM FOIL

SOIL   COMPOST   SAND

A FEW EARTHWORMS

DEAD LEAVES AND VEGETABLE SCRAPS

1 Get an adult to cut around the bottle just below the top.

← CUT HERE

2 SLIT ↓ Cut a short slit in the side then fill the bottle with layers of soil, sand, and compost.

SOIL →
SAND →
COMPOST →

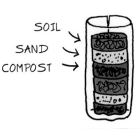

3 Dig up three or four worms from your garden. Add them to the bottle and see how quickly they burrow out of sight!

4 Add dead leaves for food on top, plus a little cold water. Put the top back on the bottle, then wrap it in foil. Worms don't like the light!

5 Give them a day or so to settle in, then peel back the foil. You should see worms in burrows.

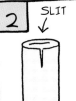

6 Feed and water your worms for a week and see what they do to the layers.

Close the foil after peeking!

7 Then return the worms to your garden.

Home sweet home!

JOHN JAMES AUDUBON
"HIGH-FLYING ORNITHOLOGIST*"

BORN:
1785, Haiti
DIED:
1851, USA

Hi! I'm John James Audubon, one of the world's greatest wildlife artists!

*Ornithologists study birds.

In 1820, I set out to find and paint all the birds of the USA!

Coo!

All 435 species, lifesize and in color. Phew!

Sadly, this meant shooting some of the specimens so he could draw them.

Behind you!

Bah!

Some of the dead birds took so long to draw that they turned rotten.

This stinks!

I agree.

But in the end, he recorded all 435—though some he had to bend a bit to fit on the page...

FLAMINGO

← SWAN

← HERON

Audubon also discovered 25 new species!

My book "Birds of America" was massive—literally!

PROUD!

OVER 3 FEET (1 M) HIGH!

In 2010, a first edition of my book sold for over $10 million! A world record for a book about nature!

Coo, again!

Luckily you can get a modern guide for far less and begin studying birds yourself!

Or try a library! See you soon!

Audubon had to hunt for his specimens.
Build a feeder and bring the birds to you!

FEED THE BIRDS

Birds are a great way to start studying nature. Many species can be tempted into your garden with food.

Make some simple seed feeders and you can study them close-up as they stuff their beaks.

 ~ Yum!

You will need:

CLEAN RECYCLABLE DRINK CONTAINERS

STICKS

SHARP SCISSORS (TAKE CARE!)

STRING

BIRD SEED

1

This basic method works for most drink bottles and cartons. First, ask an adult to help you make a few small holes in the base using the tips of the scissors.

↑↑ ↑↑
DRAINAGE HOLES

2

Next, ask an adult to make a hole just large enough to take a stick, then repeat on the opposite side of the container.

3

CUT OUT
CUT OUT
CUT OUT

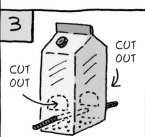

Insert a stick to make a perch, then cut out feeding holes on both sides.

4

HOLE
HOLE
HOLE

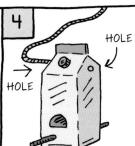

Make holes on either side, then thread through some string for hanging.

5

Fill the feeder with seed using a funnel or paper cone, then hang in a safe place outdoors, away from cats.

Wash and recycle old feeders!

PRINT A PLANT

Jane Colden

☆ Jane Colden (1724–1766) was a pioneering American plant hunter. She recorded the details of over 300 wild plants growing near her home in New York state, 250 years ago.

☆ Jane also drew and took prints of their leaves, giving us the only record we have today of what native plants once grew there. Try making leaf prints yourself.

HOW TO MAKE A LEAF PRINT

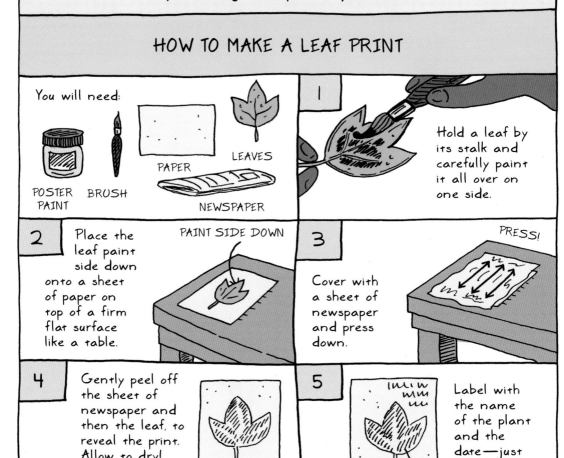

You will need:

POSTER PAINT   BRUSH   PAPER   LEAVES   NEWSPAPER

1 Hold a leaf by its stalk and carefully paint it all over on one side.

2 Place the leaf paint side down onto a sheet of paper on top of a firm flat surface like a table.

PAINT SIDE DOWN

3 Cover with a sheet of newspaper and press down.

PRESS!

4 Gently peel off the sheet of newspaper and then the leaf, to reveal the print. Allow to dry!

5 Label with the name of the plant and the date—just like Jane Colden did!

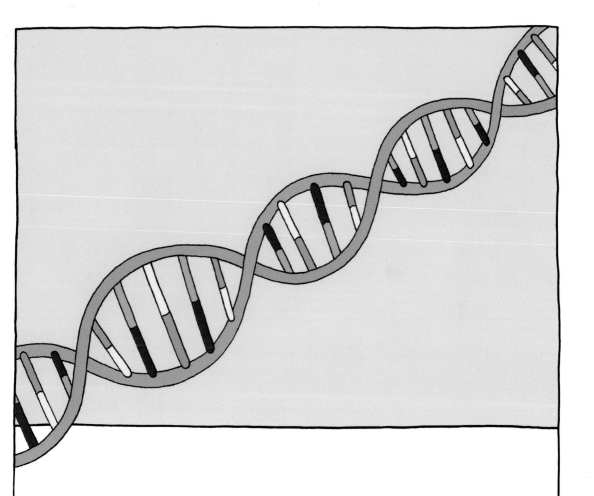

HUMAN BIOLOGY

Experiment on the most amazing
subject there is—YOU!

JAN EVANGELISTA PURKYNĚ
"HANDS-ON SCIENTIST"

BORN:
1787, Czech Republic
DIED:
1869, Czech Republic

Hi! I'm Jan Purkyně (pur-ki-ner). Heard of me?

Probably not...but that's okay. I was once so famous that people sent me letters simply addressed like this...

Purkyně,
Europe

And those letters still reached me! Hooray! More fan mail!

Anyway, I trained as a doctor and I have lots of things named after me.

FIBERS IN
THE HEART

CELLS IN
THE BRAIN

BLOOD
VESSELS
IN THE EYE

I also discovered sweat glands... What's causing this stink?

WHIFF!

However, here's a "handy" clue to my most famous achievement.

....to name just a few!

I was the first person to define the nine types of fingerprints!

Today, fingerprints are important in crime solving and cyber-security.

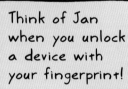

Think of Jan when you unlock a device with your fingerprint!

Thanks, Jan!

Jan Purkyně was one of a kind. Now check out your own unique fingerprints!

PRINT DETECTIVE

☆ The study of fingerprints is called "dactyloscopy."

☆ The ridges on our fingers actually help us to grip things more securely.

☆ No two people have the same fingerprints—not even identical twins!

✓ Learn how to take fingerprints with this unique activity.

☆ Here are some of Jan's fingerprint patterns.

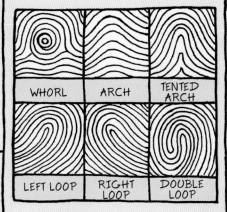

| WHORL | ARCH | TENTED ARCH |
| LEFT LOOP | RIGHT LOOP | DOUBLE LOOP |

You will need:

TAPE

SOFT LEAD PENCIL —2B OR SOFTER

WHITE PAPER

1 Use the pencil to create a dark patch on the paper.

2 Roll a fingertip over the dark patch.

3 Press the fingertip onto the sticky surface of a strip of tape.

4  Stick the print onto another sheet of paper and repeat for all your fingers.

5 Label the different fingers and use a magnifying glass to compare them to the patterns shown above!

Fingerprint your family and friends. Do some patterns seem more common than others? ❓

HERMANN VON HELMHOLTZ
"VISIONARY SCIENTIST"

BORN: 1821, Germany
DIED: 1894, Germany

Hello! My name is Hermann von Helmholtz.

As a scientist, I investigated lots of things—sound, energy, forces...

ZAP!

But I also looked into human eyes.

THE EYE

In fact, I invented a special tool for doing just that!

THE OPHTHALMOSCOPE

I used it to find out new things about vision...

...some of which you can see for yourself in these simple experiments!

OPTICAL TRICKS

1 Every eye has a "blind spot" where images are not registered. Here's how to find yours.

+

Close your right eye and focus on the cross above with your left. Slowly bring the book closer to your face from arm's length. At some point the eyeball will "vanish" when it hits your "blind spot."

2 Because eyes have "blind spots," the brain compensates by filling in the gaps.

+

Repeat the viewing method above and this time you should find the gap in the bar suddenly disappears. Your brain is making things up!

Using my new ophthalmoscope, I discovered special cells in our eyes called "cones" that register the colors red, blue, and green.

These cones get tired if stimulated for too long and produce ghostly "after-images" in false colors.

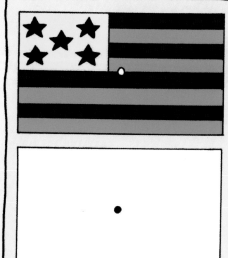

3 Stare at the dot in the top flag for 20 seconds, then look at the dot in the white box below. A very different looking flag appears.

4 Each of your eyes sends a separate image to your brain. Your brain then combines them into a single picture— as below!

Roll a sheet of paper into a tube and hold it up to your right eye. Then hold your left hand in front of you, touching the tube. Look straight ahead with both eyes open and your hand will seem to have a hole in it!

5 Having two eyes, each viewing the world from a slightly different position, helps us to judge distances more easily—as this experiment will show you!

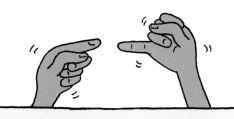

Close one eye, then try to touch the tip of your right index finger and the tip of your left little finger. With one eye closed, it's not easy. With both open, it's simple!

☆ Optical illusions are proof that serious science can also be great fun. Many are created by scientists investigating how our brains work and are often named after them.

For example, the crazy shape shown here is called a "Penrose triangle" after its inventor, Roger Penrose (born UK, 1931).

Could you actually construct this thing?

 Try these classic optical illusions yourself, then test your family and friends. Answers are given upside down at the end, but no cheating!

1	GOING BANANAS	2	TIP-TOP TABLE TOPS

Which banana is biggest, A or B?

A   B

Which table is the longest?

A   B

3	ON A PLATE

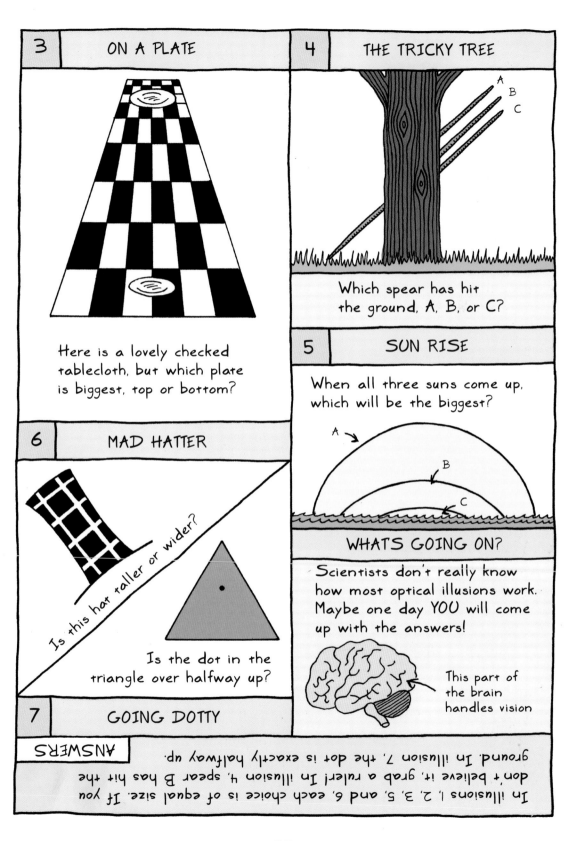

Here is a lovely checked tablecloth, but which plate is biggest, top or bottom?

6	MAD HATTER

Is this hat taller or wider?

Is the dot in the triangle over halfway up?

7	GOING DOTTY

4	THE TRICKY TREE

Which spear has hit the ground, A, B, or C?

5	SUN RISE

When all three suns come up, which will be the biggest?

WHATS GOING ON?

Scientists don't really know how most optical illusions work. Maybe one day YOU will come up with the answers!

This part of the brain handles vision

ANSWERS

In illusions 1, 2, 3, 5, and 6, each choice is of equal size. If you don't believe it, grab a ruler! In illusion 4, spear B has hit the ground. In illusion 7, the dot is exactly halfway up.

ROSALIND FRANKLIN
"DNA DETECTIVE"

BORN:
1920, England
DIED:
1958, England

 Rosalind Franklin was a skilled chemist whose work helped reveal the structure of DNA, the chemical blueprint for all living things, including you!

Rosalind Franklin

 DNA (Deoxyribonucleic Acid) is a long molecule found in cells that carries the code for how an organism is constructed.

 Rosalind X-rayed strands of DNA and her photographs showed the molecule was shaped like a long twisted ladder (a "double-helix").

 Rosalind's work was historic but sadly she died before she could be properly honored for it.

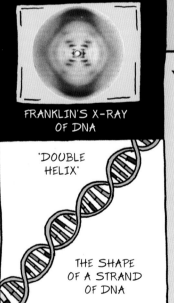
FRANKLIN'S X-RAY OF DNA

"DOUBLE HELIX"

THE SHAPE OF A STRAND OF DNA

 DIy DNA

 The next page shows you how to extract DNA at home from the cells of strawberries!

! Get a grown-up to help. Work on a sheet of old newspaper in case of spills and keep the alcohol away from your eyes or any naked flames.

You will need:

SMALL CLEAN GLASS JAR

SALT

DISHWASHING LIQUID

PAPERCLIP

TEASPOON

SMALL SIEVE

SEALABLE PLASTIC BAGS

FRESH STRAWBERRIES

SMALL BOTTLE OF RUBBING ALCOHOL/ SURGICAL SPIRIT (FROM DRUGSTORE)

1. Begin by placing the bottle of alcohol in the freezer for 30 minutes. (It works best when cold.)

2. Half-fill the jar with cold water. Add a teaspoon of salt, two teaspoons of dishwashing liquid, and stir to dissolve.

3. Pop two or three strawberries into the bag and add the mixture from the jar. Seal the bag so it will not leak.

4. Squish all the strawberries so they become a pink mush. (Do this on top of some newspaper.)

SQUISH!

5. Pour the contents of the bag into the jar through the small sieve.

6. Press the pulp with a spoon then remove the sieve and add two teaspoons of cold alcohol to the jar.

7. A thin layer of white strands should form on top of the pink liquid. This is DNA!

WHITE STRANDS

PINK LIQUID

8. You can hook out the DNA with an opened paperclip and dry it on some tissue to examine it!

✓ Pour the contents of the jar down the sink afterward, then rinse the jar and recycle it.

A QUESTION OF TASTE

 For almost a century, people were told that specific areas of the tongue each detected just one of the five tastes shown in this "tongue map" on the right.

 We now know this is wrong! Tastebuds—tiny taste receptors—can detect all of the tastes all over your tongue—and you can prove this at home!

This is wrong!

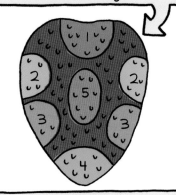

1. Bitter 2. Sour 3. Salty
4. Sweet 5. Umami (savory)

TEST YOUR TASTEBUDS

You will need:

  3 BOWLS

SUGAR

 COTTON SWABS (NON-PLASTIC)

SALT

VINEGAR

FRESH WATER

1 Three tastes are very easy to test. Pour a little water into each of the bowls, then add salt to one, sugar to another, and vinegar to the third. These are your "salty," "sweet," and "sour" testing solutions.

2 Stick out your tongue in front of a mirror!

3 Place one cotton swab in one solution, then touch it to your tongue.

Be gentle!

4 Try each solution in turn all over your tongue. Can you taste salty, sweet, and sour in every spot?

Many people still believe the false "tongue map" is correct. Ask your parents and teachers, then let them in on the tasty truth!

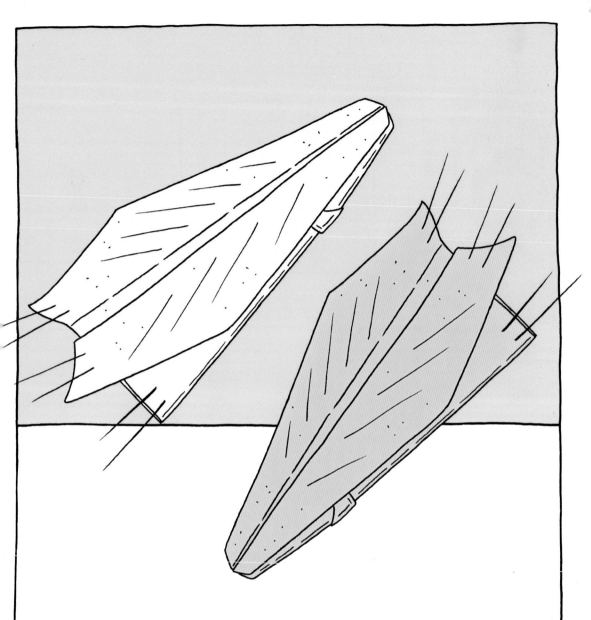

MATERIALS

From strong metals to gooey slime,
and everything in between.

FRITZ KLATTE
"POLYMER PIONEER"

BORN:
1880, Germany
DIED:
1934, Germany

Hello. My name is Fritz Klatte and I'm a cunning chemist!

In 1912 I discovered an amazing molecule—one that you use today in glues!*

* Glues such as white glue, wood glue, school glue and "Elmer's glue."

This molecule is called vinyl acetate.

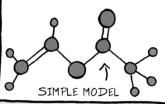

SIMPLE MODEL

Hydrogen atom
Carbon atom
Oxygen atom

The amazing thing about vinyl acetate is that it can link up with other vinyl acetate molecules to form long chains—like me holding hands with lots of copies of me!

That's right   Yes!   True!

Molecules that form into long chains are called "polymers."

I knew that!

These polymers are used in white glues, often called "PVA."

"PVA" stands for "PolyVinyl Acetate."

Amazingly, as PVA glue dries, those long chains of molecules form a type of plastic. Oops!

STUCK!

But, best of all, you can use PVA glue to make slime...Hooray!

Fritz pioneered the science of polymers. Now use PVA to make slime!

SLIME TIME!

 Here's a simple and safe way to make slime at home!

 Adding a special ingredient (here, laundry starch) links all the long chains of PVA molecules into a fun, squishy lump!

You will need:

SMALL BOWL

FOOD COLORING

LAUNDRY STARCH

TABLESPOON

PVA GLUE

1 Half-fill a small bowl with clean, cold water. It's time to make slime!

2 Add at least five tablespoons of laundry starch and stir so the mixture looks like watery milk.

3 Add a few drops of food coloring (just for color), then add PVA glue to the bowl. Use plenty!

4 Work the mixture with your hands until a big, squishy lump forms.

5 Take out the squishy lump and pour away the excess liquid. Congratulations— you've made slime!

SLIME!

6 Slime is strange stuff! It seems solid when you squeeze it, but it is actually still a liquid and will spread on a plate!

SQUEEZE!

SQUISH!

Your slime will keep for weeks in a container in the fridge!

HANS CHRISTIAN OERSTED
"METAL DETECTOR"

BORN:
1777, Denmark
DIED:
1851, Denmark

Hans Christian Oersted was a Danish super-scientist.

Hi!

GREAT DANE

ALSO A GREAT DANE

Woof!

As a child, Hans was chemistry-mad and wanted to be a scientist when he grew up.

YOUNG HANS

If I can survive that long... CHOKE!

Don't try this at home!

The adult Hans was interested in all sorts of experimenting.

I was particularly attracted to magnets!

Hans made many new discoveries, including the chemical (piperine) that makes pepper hot!

An achievement not to be sneezed at. AH-CHOO!

Hans also made history when he isolated another kitchen essential...

Need a clue?

Yes! In 1825, Hans went and discovered aluminum!

Al

No one had seen the actual metal before. It doesn't exist in nature!

Hans only made a tiny amount...

But it was rarer than gold!

Woof!*

* Translation: Wow!

Nowadays, this strong but light metal plays a massive role in our lives.

PHONES   LAPTOPS   PACKAGING

In fact, you could say aluminum is everywhere.

ZOOM!

Including up there!

Modern jet planes are up to 80 percent aluminum! Now make and fly your own aluminum aircraft!

FLIGHT TEST

⭐ Aluminum is amazing! Light and strong, it doesn't rust or generate sparks, making it an ideal material for aircraft and spacecraft.

You will need:

SHEETS OF PRINTER PAPER

ALUMINUM FOIL

SCISSORS

✔ But is aluminum better than simple paper for making darts to fly at home?

✔ Follow these instructions to fold a dart from a sheet of paper and another from a sheet of foil cut to the same size. Then try flying them!

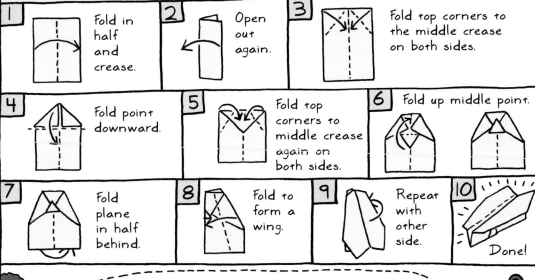

1. Fold in half and crease.

2. Open out again.

3. Fold top corners to the middle crease on both sides.

4. Fold point downward.

5. Fold top corners to middle crease again on both sides.

6. Fold up middle point.

7. Fold plane in half behind.

8. Fold to form a wing.

9. Repeat with other side.

10. Done!

Which plane flies farthest?
Which is easiest to adjust?
Which plane is more easily damaged?
Which plane uses cheaper materials?

✔ Recycle your planes when you have finished!

SOREN SORENSEN
"COLORFUL CHEMIST"

BORN:
1868, Denmark
DIED:
1939, Denmark

Hello! I'm Soren Sorensen and, like Hans Oersted (page 30), I'm also a chemist, and another great Dane!

In 1909, I was running probably the finest laboratory in the world —one inside a brewery making beer. Cheers!

Helping me in my work was my wife Margrethe...

Who are you talking to, Soren?

Making good beer is all about taste, of course (see page 26).

Have you gone mad, darling?

So, I needed an accurate, scientific way to indicate just how sour or bitter something was.

Perhaps it's the beer fumes?

Sour things like lemon juice are acids, while many bitter tastes are due to alkalis.*

LEMON = SOUR
BROCCOLI = BITTER

* These are also known as "bases."

0	1	2	3	4	5	6	7	8	9	10	11	12	13

To help chemists, I invented a colored scale* that ran from "0" (very acidic) to "14" (very alkaline).

Seriously, who are you talking to?

* called the "pH scale."

Pure water is not acidic or alkaline. It's neutral and has a pH of 7.

Yes, well, I'd stick to water for now, if I were you...

Now make your own acid/alkali indicator and test lots of fluids at home!

CHAMELEON WATER

⭐ Red cabbage contains a pigment that changes across a range of colors when put in contact with acids and alkalis, similar to a pH scale.

✓ Here's how to make your own color-changing "chameleon water" indicator!

You will need:

RED CABBAGE LEAVES

SAUCEPAN

CLEAN JARS

SIEVE

BOWL

SCISSORS

SPOON

1 Cut several red cabbage leaves into small pieces using the scissors.

2  Place the pieces into a saucepan and get a grown-up to add enough hot water to just cover them. Take care!

3  When the water has cooled, strain the purple cabbage water through a sieve into a bowl.

4 You've made chameleon water! Now you can use it to test many substances at home. Acids turn it red/pink. Alkalis turn it blue, green, and yellow.

5 Mix water with different household substances in the jars. Spoon in some of the chameleon water and see what colors you get!

| LEMON JUICE | WHITE VINEGAR | TONIC WATER | TAP WATER | TOOTHPASTE | LAUNDRY LIQUID | WASHING POWDER |

ACIDIC (low pH) ⟵ NEUTRAL ⟶ ALKALINE (high pH)

ROBERT ANGUS SMITH
"RAIN MAN"

BORN: 1817, Scotland
DIED: 1884, Wales

Hello. I am the renowned Scottish chemist Robert Angus Smith...

...and this is an egg!

Hi

Using this egg, I will demonstrate the damaging effects of a type of pollution that I named... ACID RAIN!

Eek!

Acid rain forms when pollutants produced by burning fuels such as coal and oil react with water in the atmosphere.

Smith named it in 1872.

The rain becomes an acid that can dissolve objects made of chalk—like the shell of this egg.

Uh-oh...

You can copy this experiment yourself at home!

Please don't!

You will need:

AN EGG

GLASS

WHITE VINEGAR

1 Place the egg gently into the glass and cover it with vinegar.

Goodbye! (SOB!)

2 Immediately the acid in the vinegar reacts with the chalky eggshell making lots of bubbles!

— BUBBLES

3 The bubbles are carbon dioxide gas (CO_2). Eventually all the shell dissolves leaving the egg floating in its membrane. Weird!

Not fair! Bah!

BEFORE

AFTER

Acid rain does the same to buildings and statues!

AIR

Recreate some pretty magical
experiments with air.

OTTO VON GUERICKE
"SUCKER FOR A VACUUM"

BORN:
1602, Germany
DIED:
1686, Germany

Otto von Guericke (ger-ik-er) was a German scientist famous today for an amazing air experiment.

Ja! And it involved horses.

Neigh?

← OTTO   NOT-OTTO ↑

Otto was very interested in vacuums.

Not this sort ↑

This sort ↓

A totally empty space

At the time many people still believed what Aristotle had said ages ago.

Nothing, by definition, cannot exist. So there!

But he was wrong!

To prove Aristotle wrong, Otto invented the first ever vacuum pump!

Aristotle's idea sucks. This pump does too, but in a good way!

(ABOUT 1650)

Using his vacuum pump, Otto began sucking the air out of all sorts of containers.

Do you believe in vacuums?

Nah! I think there's nothing in them...

PULL!   SUCK!

Interestingly, Otto discovered that an alarm clock inside a vacuum couldn't be heard chiming.

That's striking! Or is it?

SILENCE

Read about sound on page 60.

Otto then hit upon his most famous experiment, known as the "Magdeburg hemispheres*."

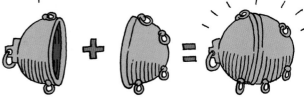

Otto made two hollow halves of a heavy brass sphere, 20 inches (50 cm) across.

* named after the town where he lived

UNDER PRESSURE

✓ You can carry out your own mini version of Otto's experiment using two toy arrows with safety suckers on their tips. Squash them together, then try to pull them apart. It's not easy!

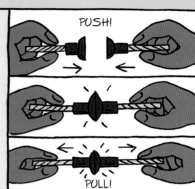

PUSH!

POLL!

☆ Air pressure is the weight (mass) of the atmosphere pressing down on the surface of a thing.

✓ Even though you can't see, taste, or touch air, here's one simple way to prove it has mass.

You will need:

THIN STRIP OF WOOD OR STIFF CARDBOARD, ABOUT 12 INCHES (30 CM) LONG

12 INCHES (30 CM) OF THIN STRING

TWO IDENTICAL BALLOONS

TAPE

1

Tape an uninflated balloon to each end of your wood.

2

Tie the string in the center so it balances and hangs level.

3

Carefully remove one balloon. Blow it up, knot it, and then tape it back in place on the wood.

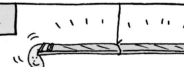

The blown-up balloon tips the balance downward, proving air has mass!

Here's another experiment to demonstrate air pressure.

You will need:

SHEET OF NEWSPAPER
ABOUT 24 X 16 INCHES
(60 X 40 CM)

THIN STRIP OF WOOD
OR STIFF CARDBOARD

TABLE OR OTHER
FLAT SURFACE

1  Place the wood so that it overhangs the table edge.

2  Cover the wood with the sheet of newspaper and smooth it down flat.

3  Strike the overhanging end of the wood with your hand (take care!).

What happens? The paper stays put, but the strip bends or breaks. The air pressing down on the sheet of paper is roughly equal to the weight of a rhinoceros! This keeps it in place.

This next air pressure experiment is amazing. You could say it is a "glass act!" Do you dare?

You will need:

HALF-FULL GLASS
OF COLD WATER

SQUARE OF STIFF CARDBOARD
(BIG ENOUGH TO COVER THE GLASS)

COURAGE (OPTIONAL)

1 Place the cardboard over the top of the glass.

2  Holding the cardboard in place, turn everything upside down.

3  Let go of the cardboard. It should stay in place due to air pressure!

AIR PRESSURE

4  Do you dare to do this? Really? Go for it!

DANIEL BERNOULLI
"MAN OF PRINCIPLE"

BORN:
1700, Netherlands
DIED:
1782, Switzerland

Hello. My name is Daniel Bernoulli— and I was just one of many clever members of my family.

For example, my Dad* was also a mathematician and a scientist.

* JOHANN BERNOULLI (1667–1748)

However, he was so jealous of my talents as a child that he tried to stop me from studying science!

Stop it!

No!

Well, it didn't work, and today it's ME that has a famous scientific principle* named after them!

GRR!

* Bernoulli's principle

This principle I shall now show in action using a hair dryer and a ping-pong ball.

DRIER

TABLE TENNIS BALL

With the hair dryer on a cold setting, I put the ball in the stream of air, and....

"◯"

WHIRRR!

...hey presto!

"◯"

HOVER! WHIRRR!

The ball hovers above the dryer, even if you move it around!

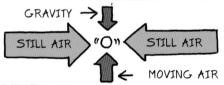

GRAVITY →

STILL AIR → "◯" ← STILL AIR

← MOVING AIR

Why? Well, Bernoulli's principle says the moving air under the ball exerts a lower pressure than the still air on either side of it (see page 37).

The still air "pushes" the ball to keep it always in place above the dryer. What do you think, Dad?

Stop it!

"◯"

You can demonstrate Bernoulli's principle easily at home. Try these fun tricks!

GO WITH THE FLOW

☆ Bernoulli's principle states that moving air exerts a lower pressure than still, non-moving air.

✓ Each of these experiments shows Dan's principle in action—with the answers given upside down at the bottom. No peeking!

1 BALLOON-ACY

Blow here

Inflate two balloons, tie them on strings, and then hang them slightly apart. Blow between them. What happens?

2 WHAT A BLOW!

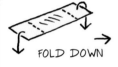

FOLD DOWN → BLOW!

Fold a paper strip into a simple bridge. Place it on a flat surface and blow steadily under the bridge. What happens?

3 NARROW SQUEAK

Cut out a V-shaped notch

Blow hard in here!

Fold another paper strip and cut out a notch to make this squeaker, as shown. Place it between two fingers and blow hard. What happens?

4 KEEP IT UP

FLOAT!   HOVER!

MARBLE

COLD AIR →

Place a marble inside a balloon, inflate it, and knot the end. What happens?

ANSWERS

1. The balloons are pushed together by the greater air pressure on the outer sides. 2. The bridge is flattened by the greater air pressure above it. 3. The squeaker makes an awful noise, all thanks to Bernoulli's principle! 4. The balloon and marble work just like the ping-pong ball on page 40.

41

THE WRIGHT BROTHERS
"FLIGHT BROTHERS"

Hello. I'm American flying legend Wilbur Wright...

BORN: USA, 1867
DIED: USA, 1912

...and this is my baby brother, Orville—also a legend, of course.

Hi

BORN: USA, 1871
DIED: USA, 1948

Orv and I built bicycles before we got interested in flying machines.

True!

That all started when a great German aviation pioneer* crashed his glider and died.

Oh dear! Moving on...

OTTO

* OTTO LILIENTHAL (1848–1896)

It took us seven years, but Orv and I eventually built and flew the world's first powered airplane! Orv piloted our "Wright Flyer" at Kitty Hawk, North Carolina, on December 17, 1903.

WRIGHT FLYER

WILBUR

ORVILLE

Along the way we made many model gliders and a really massive kite.

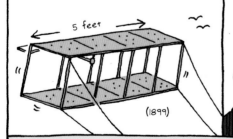

5 feet

(1899)

The kite helped us work out how to steer the Wright Flyer.

But there was just one problem...

My turn now. I wanna go! Come on!

No! Let go!

Air makes flight possible for birds, bees—and brothers! Build a kite and see for yourself!

☆ Kites are some of the oldest known manmade flying objects, dating back over 2,500 years!

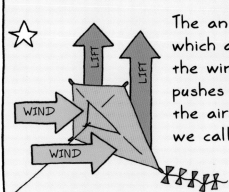

The angle at which a kite hits the wind is what pushes it up into the air—a force we call "lift."

You will need:

SKEWER (TAKE CARE!)

PRINTER-SIZE CARDSTOCK OR PAPER

 STAPLER

SMALL BIT OF TAPE

STRONG THREAD OR NYLON LINE

✓ This simple kite is made from just a single sheet of paper. Give it a try!

1

Fold the sheet of paper or cardstock in half and crease it.

2

Curl the corner down to the point that is here marked "X."

3

Staple the corner so that it stays in place, then do the same thing with the corner on the other side.

4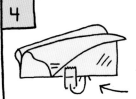

Next fold a small bit of tape over the keel at the point shown here.

5

Get a grown-up to help pierce a hole through the tape using a skewer.

6

Tie your kite to the strong thread or nylon line.

7

Fly in a light breeze. Simple!

WIND ⟶

WIND ⟶

It needs no tail!

JAMES CLERK MAXWELL
"THE GREAT MAXO"

BORN:
1831, Scotland
DIED:
1879, England

Hello. I'm the usually serious scientist James Clerk Maxwell, but today you can call me...

"The Great Maxo!"

I'm about to show you a simple trick. It demonstrates an important scientific theory that I helped develop!

Namely, I shall submerge this paper tissue under water without it becoming wet!

Impossible, surely?

First, I take out from inside my beard...

...a glass! VOILA!

Next, I press a tissue firmly up into the bottom of the glass.

TISSUE

PUSH!

Now, I simply push the glass upside down into this tank of cold water...

AIR

WATER

Trapped air keeps the tissue dry!

This happens because air is a mix of gas molecules that resist being squashed together!

AIR MOLECULES

WATER MOLECULES

They push back!

Scientists call this the Kinetic Theory of Gases....

But we call it magic!

Grab a glass and give this a try yourself. You can even do it while taking a bath!

44

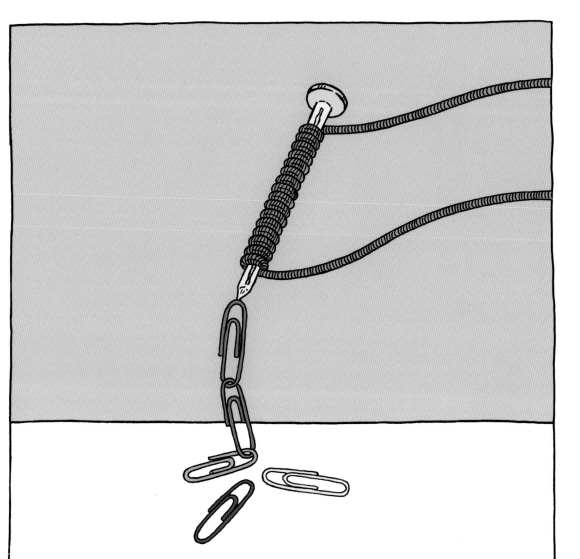

ELECTRICITY AND MAGNETISM

Learn some pretty hair-raising
science with these experiments.

ELECTRIFYING!

⭐ Around 585BCE, an ancient Greek scholar named Thales of Miletus found that rubbing fur onto a lump of amber (fossilized tree resin) left the amber with the ability to attract hair and feathers. Why?

✓ Copy these simple experiments and see this strange effect for yourself! Answers are upside down below.

Thales

1 Rub an inflated balloon many times in the same direction on your clothes, then hold it against a wall. What happens?

2 Rub the balloon on your clothes again, then hold it over some tiny scraps of paper and a mixture of ground pepper and salt. What happens?

PAPER SCRAPS

PEPPER AND SALT

3 Once again, rub the balloon on your clothes. Now bring it close to a gentle, thin stream of water. What do you see this time?

4 Charge up the balloon again, then bring it close to an empty aluminum drink can on a flat surface. Can you control the can?

ANSWERS

1. The balloon clings to the wall. 2. The balloon attracts the paper and the pepper. 3. The balloon bends the stream of water. 4. Yes, you can!

⭐ Thales had discovered "static electricity." Rubbing the amber (like the balloon) left it with an electric charge like a lightning bolt!

BENJAMIN FRANKLIN
"HIGH-FLYING GUY"

BORN:
1706, USA
DIED:
1790, USA

Hello! My name is Benjamin Franklin, and I was an American scientist and inventor!

Legend has it that I flew a kite in a storm to show that lightning was a form of static electricity*.

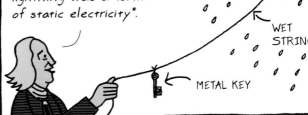

WET STRING

METAL KEY

* Franklin called it "electric fire."

Well, if I did do that, it was incredibly dangerous. Other people who tried the same thing were sadly electrocuted and died.

Never fly a kite in a storm is my advice.

KER-ACK!

Instead, stay indoors and make your own mini-lightning!

SPARKS IN THE DARK

You will need:

BALLOON

METAL SPOON

DARK ROOM

1

In a dark room, stroke the balloon many times against your hair so it builds up lots of static.

2

Now slowly bring the charged balloon close to the spoon —a spark should jump across!

The spark is a mini lightning bolt of static electricity. The crack you hear is a tiny thunderclap!

WILLIAM GILBERT
"MAGNETIC PERSONALITY MAN"

BORN: 1544, England
DIED: 1603, England

Hello. I'm William Gilbert, Elizabethan scientist and doctor, and I have something amazing under my hat...

Me!

I was one of the first scientists to insist on proving theories by experiments.

And it was me that invented the word "electricity*!"

BRIGHT SPARK

* From the Greek word "elektra," meaning amber (page 46).

But for me, the big attraction was magnets and magnetism.

GRIP!
TUG!
CLUNK!

I saw that the needles in the compasses used by sailors are actually small magnets.

And I realized that they worked because the Earth itself is a giant magnet!

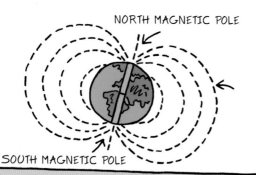

NORTH MAGNETIC POLE

SOUTH MAGNETIC POLE

I also figured out how to use one magnet to make many more!

The secret is on the next page, but try to keep it under your hat!

Attracted to the idea of making your own magnets? Come and give it a try!

Magnetism is an invisible force caused by how atoms are lined up inside certain magnetic materials.

 Only a few common metals are magnetic: iron (steel), cobalt, and nickel.

 All magnets have two 'poles': north (N) and south (S).

'ATTRACT'   'REPEL'

 Opposite poles attract, while identical poles "repel"— pushing each other away.

You will need:

A MAGNET (YOU CAN USE A FRIDGE MAGNET)

AN IRON OR STEEL BOLT OR OPENED PAPERCLIP

 EXTRA PAPERCLIPS

1 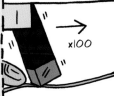 x100

Stroke the paperclip or bolt 100 times, always in the same direction.

2

Now test if it will pick up other paperclips! Try both ends!

MAKE A COMPASS

You will need:

 BOWL OF COLD WATER

SMALL PIECE OF CARDSTOCK

 MAGNETIZED PAPERCLIP

 "PROPER" COMPASS (OPTIONAL)

1 Gently float the piece of cardstock on top of the water.

2 Lay the newly magnetized paperclip on top of the cardstock.

3 The paperclip will turn so that it lines up in a north/south direction.

4 Check it with an actual compass.

 WOW!

Michael Faraday

☆ Michael Faraday (1791–1867) was a great British scientist whose discoveries paved the way for lots of modern technology.

In 1824, Faraday invented the rubber party balloon!

☆ Among his many experiments, Faraday showed how passing electricity through a wire creates a magnetic effect, which can be used to make an "electromagnet." Here's how!

You will need:

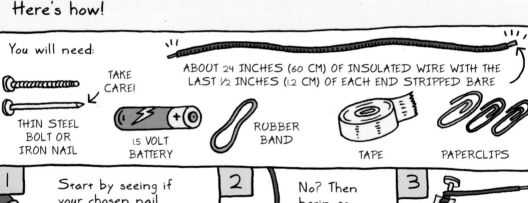

ABOUT 24 INCHES (60 CM) OF INSULATED WIRE WITH THE LAST ½ INCHES (1.2 CM) OF EACH END STRIPPED BARE

THIN STEEL BOLT OR IRON NAIL — TAKE CARE!

1.5 VOLT BATTERY

RUBBER BAND

TAPE

PAPERCLIPS

1 Start by seeing if your chosen nail or bolt will pick up metal paperclips.

2 No? Then begin to wind wire around the nail/bolt in tight coils.

3 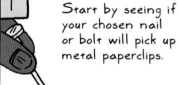 Use tape to hold the coil if needed.

4 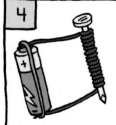 Use the rubber band to attach the bare ends of wire to the battery terminals to make a circuit.

5  Now try picking up paperclips. Does it work?

! The magnet can get warm and use lots of power, so don't leave it attached to the battery!

FORCES AND PHYSICS

Study pushes, pulls, and the laws
of physics with these experiments.

HYPATIA OF ALEXANDRIA
"THE OPPOSITE OF DENSE"

BORN: about 370BC, Egypt
DIED: 415BC, Egypt

Hello! I'm Hypatia — a brilliant mathematician, philosopher, and...

....a very popular teacher!

Hi, Hy!

Hi, Hy!

I invented a clever device called a "hydrometer."

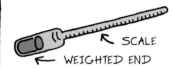

← SCALE

← WEIGHTED END

Still used today!

A hydrometer indicates the density of liquids by how far down it floats in them.

DENSER

LESS DENSE

Density depends on how much matter a liquid contains.

For example, you can make water denser by adding salt — as this fun trick will show!

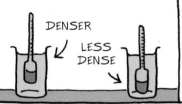

You will need:

GLASS OF WARM WATER

SPOON

SALT

Hello, again!

EGG

1 Gently place the egg in the glass of water.

Don't crack me!

2 The egg should sink to the bottom because it is denser than pure water.

Who are you calling dense?

3 Now start adding salt to the water, stirring gently to dissolve it.

Yuk! Salty!

4 Eventually, the salty water's density equals that of the egg and...

(It will take several spoonfuls.)

5 ...the egg will just hang in the middle of the glass! Wow!

This egg-speriment is fun (for once)!

ARCHIMEDES
"MAN OF THE MOMENT"

BORN:
about 287 BCE, Greece
DIED:
about 212 BCE, Greece

Hello! My name is Archimedes. I was yet another ancient Greek thinker.

Often my best ideas came to me in the bath....

Must get a bigger bathtub!

Including my famous "Eureka" moment...EUREKA!

"Eureka" is Greek for "I have found it!"

I had been asked by a king to find the volume of an odd-shaped crown.

Supposedly solid gold!

I was stumped until I realized the bath water rose when I sat in it!

Without me | With me

The water rose by the same volume as the part of me in the bath!

Well, after shouting "Eureka!," the story goes that I ran around naked!

True or not, here's how to use the same method to work out your own volume!

You will need:

WAX CRAYON

MEASURING CUP

BATH

1 Run a bath. Before you get in, mark the starting water level with the wax crayon.

(Wax wipes off!)

2 Now get in. Lie low in the bath and mark the new level of the water.

3 After your bath, the volume of your body is equal to the number of cups of water it takes to raise the bath level between the two marks. Measure them!

AGNES POCKELS
"KITCHEN CHEMISTRY QUEEN"

BORN:
1862, Italy
DIED:
1935, Germany

Hello! I'm German chemist Agnes Pockels.

And this is my big brother Friedrich.

Hello!

We were both super-interested in science as young people.

YOUNG AGNES

YOUNG FRIEDRICH

But only one of us was allowed to study science at college. Guess who...

Sorry, Agnes!

Friedrich became a professor!

I had to stay at home while Friedrich went to college. But he kindly lent me all his books.

Here you go!

So, I taught myself science, but I also had to do a lot of housework, like washing dishes!

However, through doing the dishes I became an expert on water, soaps, and oils.

Agnes investigated how they interacted.

I carried out some serious science in my kitchen and my work became world-renowned.

So, the lesson here is "never ever give up!"

And help with the dishes!

Agnes pioneered the scientific study of the surfaces of liquids. Now it's your turn!

WATER WIZARDRY!

 Agnes was very interested in the "surface tension" of water.

 "Surface tension" is where water molecules link together to form a sort of "skin" on the surface of water.

 Try these fun experiments and you can see "surface tension" in action for yourself!

FILL H:

1 Fill a glass of water to the very top. Could it possibly hold any more?

2 Yes! Carefully slip coins into the water, one by one.

3 Look from the side. The water bulges above the rim: "surface tension" in action!

SUPPORTING ROLE

 Surface tension is strong enough to support a pin or a paperclip.

SHARP! TAKE CARE!

1 Fill a shallow saucer with cold water.

2 Place a small piece of tissue paper onto the water then lay the pin/paperclip gently on top.

3 The tissue soaks up water and falls away to leave the pin/paperclip floating on the "skin." Wow!

EVERYBODY SCATTER!

 Soaps and dishwashing liquids work by weakening the links between water molecules. Here's how to see this in action!

1 Sprinkle some pepper over a saucerful of clean water.

2 Dip the tip of your finger into some soap or dishwashing liquid, then into the surface of the water. What happens?

ANSWER

The pepper is pulled to the edges of the saucer due to the differences in surface tension!

LAURA BASSI
"FIRST LADY OF PHYSICS"

BORN:
1711, Italy
DIED:
1778, Italy

This is Italian physicist Laura Bassi.

ADULT LAURA

Hi!

Laura loved science from a young age.

YOUNG LAURA

But there was a teensy-weensy problem...

Girls weren't allowed to study science at school!

Luckily, I had a cunning plan!

TEENAGE LAURA

Laura studied science at home instead!

At just 21 years old, Laura was made a professor of anatomy at Bologna university.

Loved the award, less so the hat!

The public went crazy and poems were written about her!

POET

O, Laura Bassi, You are so very classy!

Oof!

However, because she was a woman, the university wouldn't let Laura teach students!

So, I set up my own school at home, (of course)!

Laura taught students the new theories of English physicist Isaac Newton (see next page).

ISAAC

What a hero!

This annoyed some university colleagues who didn't agree with Newton's ideas.

WRONG

What a zero!

But, Laura won them over and in 1776 became the world's first female professor of physics.

And I now have a school named after me!

 Laura loved Isaac Newton's new ideas about how things moved. Now find out more!

ISAAC NEWTON
'FIRST CELEBRITY SCIENTIST'

BORN:
1642, England
DIED:
1727, England

Isaac Newton

☆ Isaac Newton was a great scientist who investigated many things, including light, forces (pushes and pulls), and objects in motion.

✓ These experiments are based on Isaac's ideas and are just like those Laura Bassi would have shared with her students!

STAY OR GO?

☆ Stationary objects need a push or pull to get them going. Moving objects need a push or pull to get them to stop or change direction. Obvious, yes?

☆ This resistance to change is called inertia (in-er-shah).

☆ Inertia is why we wear seatbelts in case our car stops suddenly. You can also use inertia to amaze your friends with these fab tricks!

1 You will need:

PLAYING CARD

FINGER   COIN

Balance a playing card on the tip of your finger as shown. Place a coin on top then swiftly flick away the card horizontally. What happens to the coin? Try it!

2 You will need:

 A COLD HARD-BOILED EGG

 A RAW UNCOOKED EGG

Lay both eggs on their sides and spin them with your fingers. Now stop each egg in turn with a fingertip. The raw egg will start moving again as inertia means its insides are still spinning!

3 You will need:

CHECKERS PLAYING PIECES

RULER

NERVES OF STEEL!

Pile the playing pieces as shown here. Next bring the ruler close and swiftly strike out the piece ← one up from the base. Do you dare? What happens?

4 You will need:

COINS

ARM

Do this outside! Place a small stack of coins near your elbow. Swiftly bring down your hand and try to catch them. Can you do it? Inertia says, "YES!"

SNATCH!

FEEL THE FORCE!

☆ Newton said that every action (push or pull force) had an equal and opposite reaction. Give it a try!

1 While standing on a skateboard or sitting in an office chair with wheels, push against a solid wall. What moves, and in what direction?

2 Here's how to defy gravity —the force that makes thing fall. Go outside and rapidly swing a half-full bucket of water in a vertical circle. The water stays in!

PASS IT ON!

☆ Moving objects possess an energy that they can pass on to other objects if they collide with them. Called "momentum," here are some great ways to see it in action!

1 COINS TOUCHING → Place three coins as shown on a smooth, flat surface.

Pressing firmly on the middle coin, flick the right-hand coin to hit it.

You should see the left-hand coin go flying off!

Experiment with your own combinations of extra coins!

2 ⭐ Marbles are magic for demonstrating momentum! Give this experiment a try!

You will need:

TWO RULERS

GLASS MARBLES

"VALLEY" — Place the rulers side by side to form a "valley."

Line up several marbles so that they are just touching, with one marble sat on its own.

Flick the solo marble so it hits the group. What happens?

Experiment with lots of different combinations of marbles—pushing two or more at the group. Momentum is marvelous!

These marbles are a simple version of a scientific toy called "Newton's Cradle," named after Isaac.

3 ⭐ While the game itself is great fun, this is probably the most exciting thing you can do with a box of dominoes. Give it a try!

Stand all 28 dominoes in a line, about an inch (2.5 cm) apart, then push the end one.

PUSH!

As they topple over, each domino transfers its momentum to its neighbor.

The world record for domino-toppling stands at over 76,000 dominoes!

ROUGH STUFF!

⭐ Newton noted that rough surfaces slowed down moving objects—a force we call "friction."

Try this clever friction trick! Place your hands under a long ruler or cardboard tube. Bring them slowly together and, thanks to friction, they always meet in the middle.

BELL AND EDISON
"THE BOYS OF NOISE"

Hello! I'm Alexander Graham Bell—and I invented the telephone!

BORN: 1847, Scotland
DIED: 1922, Canada

And I'm Thomas Alva Edison—and I invented the microphone...

BORN: 1847, USA
DIED: 1931, USA

...and the phonograph, and the light bulb, and the movie camera...

SIGH!

Both Edison and myself were "big noises" in the science of sound...

MOUTHPIECE ↓

BELL'S FIRST TELEPHONE

"PHONOGRAPH" ↙

EDISON'S SOUND RECORDER

...and sound is a form of energy—isn't that right, Tom?

Sorry, I wasn't listening...

Air transmits sound energy to our ears in the form of sound waves.

DING!

DING!

If you stop those waves from entering your ears, you can't hear properly.

What?

Sounds will also travel through other substances such as a table top. Try it!

Ooh! Weird!

TAP! TAP!

I love sounds! What do you say, Tom?

I should have invented earplugs!

DRUM!

Bell and Edison revolutionized modern communications. Now make some noise yourself!

→

MAKING WAVES

⭐ Alexander Graham Bell invented his electric telephone in 1876.

✓ You can send your own sound waves many feet using just a pair of yogurt tubs and some string—no batteries required!

You will need:

A PAIR OF CLEAN YOGURT TUBS OR PLASTIC/PAPER CUPS

THIN STRING OR NYLON LINE

SHARP SKEWER (TAKE CARE!)

1 With a grown-up's help, pierce a hole in the bottom of each tub using the skewer.

IN THE CENTER

2 Insert the string through the hole in one tub and tie a big knot that won't pull through.

3 Unravel 16–32 feet (5–10 m) of string and repeat step 2 with the other tub.

4 Have a friend hold one tub to their ear while you speak into the other.

Always keep the string tight!

5 At the far end, the tub acts as a loudspeaker, reproducing your voice!

6 Take turns to speak or listen— saying "over" when you stop talking.

Over!

7 Wind the string around a post to talk around corners.

Keep it tight!

The sound energy in your voice vibrates the tub, sending the sound waves along the string.

FRANK WHITTLE
"JET-SET GO-GETTER"

BORN:
1907, England
DIED:
1996, USA

Hello. I'm Frank Whittle—a small guy who had a big idea.

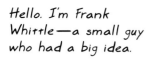

ZOOOM!

In 1930, I worked with a team to invent the jet engine!

FIRST PATENT

Jet engines work by taking in air at the front and using it to burn fuel.

BURNER

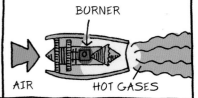

AIR   HOT GASES

AN EARLY WHITTLE JET PLANE →

ZOOOOOM!

The hot exhaust gases expand and this creates the thrust that pushes a jet plane forward!

Put simply, the gases go backward, and the plane goes forward—a form of propulsion you can copy at home with a balloon!

You will need:

BALLOON (LONG WORKS BEST)

STRONG THREAD OR NYLON LINE

CLEAN DRINKING STRAW

STRIPS OF TAPE

1 Slip the line through the straw and tie it to a firm object. Cut the line and tie the other end to a second firm object like a table.

STRAW

KEEP THE LINE TIGHT!

2 Blow up the balloon, hold it closed, and use the tape to attach it under the straw.

3 Now, let go. ZOOOOOM!

Repeat lots of times.

The energy stored in the stretched balloon skin pushes the air inside it backward so the balloon jets forward!

LIGHT

See light in a new way with
these bright experiments.

IBN AL-HAYTHAM
"ARABIAN VISIONARY"

BORN:
about 965CE, Basra, Iraq
DIED:
about 1040CE, Cairo, Egypt

Hello. My name is Ibn al-Haytham, though some also know me as "Alhazen."

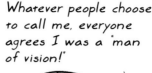

Whatever people choose to call me, everyone agrees I was a "man of vision!"

That's because I was crazy about light and sight!

Lookin' good!

Al-Haytham was very interested in reflections.

I also examined eyes to try to find out how they work.

NERVES

EYE

From one of Alhazen's drawings.

Some people claimed we could see because our eyes beamed out light rays... scary!

Help!

But I realized it was because light actually enters our eyes—when we let it...Cool, huh?!

My many experiments also proved that light travels in straight lines. Which is why we can't see around corners, sadly...

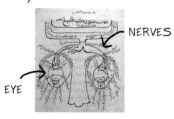

All this amazing new knowledge I then wrote up into a huge seven-volume book.

PROUD!

Called the "Book of Optics."

Don't let the title fool you—it's not "light" reading! Puff!

Al-Haytham was a very enthusiastic experimenter. Now make your own optical apparatus!

Al-Haytham studied the "camera obscura"—a small room with a hole in its wall that allowed an image of outside to be viewed as an upside-down projection indoors.

 You can make a smaller version called a "pinhole camera" easily at home!

You will need:

 SHOEBOX-SIZED CARDBOARD BOX

 SMALL PIECE OF KITCHEN FOIL

TRACING PAPER/ BAKING PARCHMENT

GLUE

SCISSORS

PIN (TAKE CARE!)

1 Cut out a small hole in the center of one end of the box and cut out a rectangle from the opposite end.

 FRONT   BACK

2 Glue a piece of kitchen foil over the small hole.

FOIL

3 Make a hole in the foil with a pin.

TAKE CARE!

4 Glue a piece of tracing paper or baking parchment over the opposite end to form a viewing screen.

 KEEP IT SMOOTH!

5 In a darkened room, point your pinhole at a brightly lit bulb.

You should see an upside-down image of the bulb on your screen.

6 The image is upside down because light travels in straight lines.

 REAL VIEW   PINHOLE   SCREEN VIEW

7 Try using your pinhole camera outside on a sunny day with a cover over your head.

 Just be careful not to bump into things!

ISAAC NEWTON
"RAINBOW WONDERER"

BORN:
1642, England
DIED:
1727, England

Hello. I'm super-scientist Isaac Newton. Welcome to my laboratory.

Dark in here, isn't it? But I am about to throw light on something amazing...

A glass prism!

HOLE IN SHUTTERS

BEAM OF SUNLIGHT

I love this experiment! The beam of light falls at an angle onto the prism...

The prism is a glass lens with a special three-sided shape.

It passes through the glass and is bent and split into bands of colors known as a "spectrum."

WHITE SCREEN

These are the same colors you see in a rainbow.

In a rainbow, raindrops act like tiny prisms.

Before me, people had some different ideas about colors...

I think colors are all blends of black and white.

← MISTAKEN PHILOSOPHER

I was the first person to show that objects look white because they reflect all the colors in the spectrum.

And this simple disc helped me to prove it!

What is the disc? Want to make your own rainbows? Just follow these instructions!

LIGHT FANTASTIC!

 Newton was right about white light being a mix of all the colors of visible light.

 Here's how to make a mini-rainbow—and how to blend the spectrum back together again!

MAKE A RAINBOW!

You will need:

 SHALLOW DISH FULL OF CLEAN WATER

 SMALL MIRROR

 FLASHLIGHT THAT GIVES A BRIGHT WHITE LIGHT

SHEET OF WHITE CARDSTOCK OR PAPER

1 | In a darkened room, rest the mirror at angle on the dish, with half of it under the water.

2 | Shine the flashlight onto the submerged part of the mirror so it reflects light up onto the cardstock. What can you see?

(upside-down text) Bands of rainbow colors should be visible.

REVERSE A RAINBOW!

The disc Isaac was holding is known as a 'Newton's Wheel'. Make and spin your own to see what it shows!

You will need:

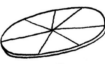 CARDSTOCK CIRCLE ABOUT 4 INCHES (10 CM) IN DIAMETER, DIVIDED INTO SEVEN EQUAL SEGMENTS

 SHORT POINTED PENCIL AND SOME COLORED PENS OR PENCILS

 SMALL PIECE OF STICKY TACK

1 | Colour the sections red, orange, yellow, green, blue, indigo and violet.

2 | With the sticky tack below, push the pencil through the center to make a top.

TAKE ← CARE!

3 | Spin it and see what happens!

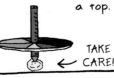

(upside-down text) The colors blend to give a 'dirty' white.

ANTONIE VAN LEEUWENHOEK
"UP CLOSE AND PERSONAL"

BORN: 1632, The Netherlands
DIED: 1723, The Netherlands

I'm Antonie van Leeuwenhoek (lee-oo-ven-huk) and I'm itching to tell you my story!

Here we go again... (SIGH)

MRS. V.L.

ANT

SCRATCH!

FLEA
Hi!

Round about 1670, I invented the microscope, but it wasn't like the ones you use today.

VERY BRIGHT

ALSO BRIGHT

ITCH!

It was very simple.

LENS

NEEDLE FOR SPECIMENS

METAL BODY

ADJUSTABLE HANDLE

But it worked!

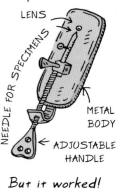

The lens was a tiny glass ball that magnified to 200 times. It was made in a way that I kept secret from everyone!

That's what he thinks!

⊙
1/8 IN
ACTUAL SIZE

I made over 500 microscopes and with them saw things no human had ever seen before!

TINY ANIMALS

SAND GRAINS

FISH SCALES

BACTERIA

REPRODUCTIVE CELLS

BLOOD CELLS

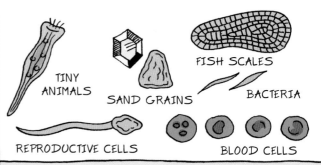

Based on actual drawings by Antonie.

I also discovered bacteria living in my own mouth! Want a look?

Yuk!

My drawings of these tiny things made me famous!

Me too! That's me, folks!

(FLEA, 1695)

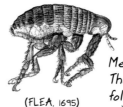

In fact, I had invented the science of microbiology!

Now, please can someone invent the toothbrush?

Microbiologists study things too small to see with the naked eye. Now, make your own magnifier! ⟶

BIG IT UP!

 Modern optical microscopes have two or more lenses to make images look larger. Van Leeuwenhoek's model had only one lens, meaning it was really just a small, but very powerful, magnifying glass!

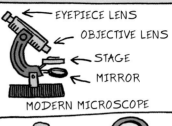

EYEPIECE LENS
OBJECTIVE LENS
STAGE
MIRROR

MODERN MICROSCOPE

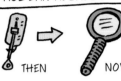

THEN   NOW

 You can make your own very simple version of a magnifying glass at home.

You will need:

SMALL PIECES OF FLAT, CLEAR PLASTIC CUT FROM A JUICE BOTTLE OR FOOD PACKAGING

COLD TAP WATER

BRIGHT LIGHT OR SUNLIGHT

1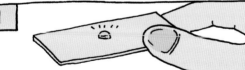

Place one small drop of cold water on a clear plastic strip.

2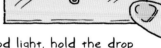

In a good light, hold the drop over what you wish to magnify. The water droplet acts as a tiny lens.

3

Bring one eye very close to the drop, so that the image comes into focus.

4

RIDGES

PRINT DOTS

With practice, you can see the ridges on your fingerprints, the dots that make up printing, and lots more!

 Amazingly, you can also see things closer up if you peer at them through a pinhole made in a piece of thin cardstock. Try it!

ALBERT EINSTEIN
"THE WIZARD OF PHYSICS"

BORN:
1879, Germany
DIED:
1955, USA

Hello. I am the great theoretical physicist Albert Einstein.

People called me a "genius"—but, honestly, with THIS hair?

However, I did do some clever things...

Like predicting the existence of black holes!

I also came up with the world's most famous scientific equation...

$$E = mc^2$$

E = energy; m = mass; c = the speed of light

I reckoned that nothing could ever travel faster than the speed of light.*

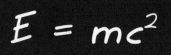

* 186,000 miles (300,000 km) per second

Even at that speed, sunlight still takes over 8 minutes to reach us!

Hurry up!

Amazingly, if you could go faster than light, then you would travel backward in time!

But surely that's impossible...isn't it?

Hello. I am the great theoretical physicist Albert Einstein.

Scientists took centuries to calculate the speed of light. You can do it at home in minutes!

MICRO-LIGHT

 Microwaves—like the light waves we get from the sun—are a form of energy that travels in invisible waves (see page 80) at the speed of light.

With the help of a grown-up, you can calculate that speed at home yourself!

You will need:

MICROWAVE OVEN

OVEN MITTS

 SHALLOW MICROWAVEABLE DISH (NON-METAL)

 BAG OF MINI-MARSHMALLOWS

 CALCULATOR

RULER IN CENTIMETERS

1 First, find the label on the oven that says the frequency it operates at—most are 2450 MHz (megahertz).

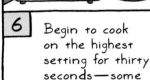

2 Write down the frequency on a piece of paper. You're on your way!

3 Take out the plate and turntable from the oven and put them in a safe place.

4 Cover the dish with a single layer of mini-marshmallows.

5 Place it inside the oven and shut the door.

6 Begin to cook on the highest setting for thirty seconds—some of them will melt!

7 Remove the dish using oven mitts and measure the distance in centimeters from the middle of one melted area to the middle of the next.

8 Write down this distance. (It will be about 6 centimeters.)

9 Now use the calculator to solve this sum:

$$\text{SPEED OF LIGHT ('c')} = \underline{\hspace{2cm}} \times \underline{\hspace{2cm}} \times 20 \text{ kilometers per second}$$

FREQUENCY (MEGAHERTZ)   DISTANCE (CM)

How close to the actual figure of 300,000 kilometers per second did you get?

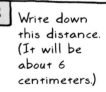

LORD RAYLEIGH
"MR. BLUE SKY"

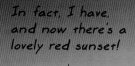

BORN:
1842, England
DIED:
1919, England

Hello. My name is John Strutt. I was made 'Lord Rayleigh' due to my work in science!

Rayleigh discovered the element argon.

Look at this blue sky—I could sit out here all day.

In fact, I have, and now there's a lovely red sunset!

Daytime skies look blue because the blue light in sunlight hits air molecules and gets deflected.

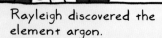

Blue gets deflected more than red or yellow light because of its shorter wavelength.

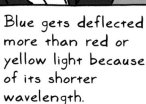

BLUE

RED

At sunset, sunlight has to travel farther. By the time it reaches our eyes, almost all of the blue has been deflected, leaving only red light. Pretty though!

This effect is called 'Rayleigh scattering,' after me—and you can show a similar effect at home!

You will need:

LARGE GLASS OF WATER

SPOONFUL OF MILK

BRIGHT FLASHLIGHT

1   Add the milk to the water and stir it well.

(It creates tiny "milk particles.")

Experiment with how much milk works best.

2   Shine the flashlight onto the glass. Viewed from the side, the milky water should look pale blue due to some blue light being scattered.

3   Now place the flashlight under the glass. Viewed from the top it should look yellowy as almost all of the blue light has been deflected away from your eyes.

Tastes awful though!

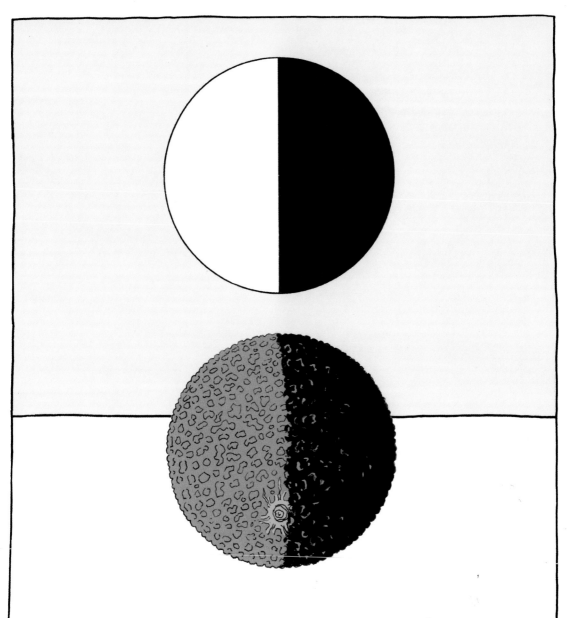

ASTRONOMY

Study the Universe with these
out-of-this world experiments.

GALILEO GALILEI
"STARGAZING SUPERSTAR"

BORN:
1564, Italy
DIED:
1642, Italy

Hello! I am the great Italian scientist and thinker Galileo!

Inside my robes I have one of the most dangerous devices invented by science...

...a telescope!

OVER 4 FEET LONG!

Galileo made his own!

This is one of my actual handmade telescopes.

EYEPIECE

FRONT LENS

(Now on display in an Italian museum!)

I didn't invent the telescope, but I was one of the first to use it to study the night sky.

FROM 1609

With it I made drawings of craters on our Moon.

And I found new moons orbiting the planet Jupiter!

By studying space, I suspected that Earth might not be the center of the Universe.

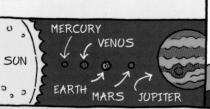
SUN
MERCURY
VENUS
EARTH MARS JUPITER

This was considered a dangerous idea, so I was made a prisoner in my own home.

Hmm...I should have seen that coming...Oh well!

Galileo was a great astronomer. Now start stargazing yourself!

STAR STRUCK!

✓ Astronomy is a great hobby —just make sure you tell a grown-up if you are going star-gazing outside in the dark, and choose a safe place like your yard.

✓ You don't need much to get started (see opposite). However, you could also make a simpler version of a telescope—like Galileo's!

You will need:

BINOCULARS ARE BETTER THAN A CHEAP TELESCOPE. '8 X 40' IS A GOOD STARTING SIZE.

BUY OR BORROW A STAR GUIDE AND TAKE A FLASHLIGHT TO READ IT!

WEAR SOMETHING WARM. IT CAN GET COLD OUTSIDE AT NIGHT!

SEEING STARS

WHAT TO SPOT

You will need:

A COUPLE OF MAGNIFYING GLASSES

☆ The night sky varies with the time of year and your location. Here are some famous "constellations"—shapes formed by groups of stars.

 Hold one magnifying glass up close to an eye and hold the other out in front of you.

2 Look at an object through both glasses, moving the second magnifier back and forth to get a focused image. What is odd about it?

What you see is upside down!

URSA MAJOR (GREAT BEAR)   CASSIOPEIA

1 | Northern hemisphere

CRUX   (SOUTHERN CROSS)   CORNUS   (THE RAVEN)

2 | Southern hemisphere

THE APOLLO 11 CREW
"LUNAR LEGENDS"

Hello. I'm the American astronaut Neil Armstrong...

BORN: 1930, USA
DIED: 2012, USA

...and this is my fellow astronaut, Edwin "Buzz" Aldrin.

Neil, you did it again!

BORN: 1930, USA

What did I do, Buzz?

You went first! First on the Moon, and first to speak to the reader!

Are you annoyed that I was the first person to set foot on the Moon?

Well...

On July 20th 1969

I also spoke those historic words, "one small step for a man, one giant leap for mankind." That was me too!

GRRR!

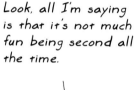

Look, all I'm saying is that it's not much fun being second all the time.

Well, I don't know what you're complaining about, Buzz!

Hey! It's Michael Collins!

BORN: 1930, Italy

I never walked on the Moon at all. I just orbited in the Apollo 11 command module.

Can't we just be happy knowing all three of us are lunar legends?

I second that!

Bah!

You don't have to go to the Moon to study it. "Moon-walk" this way!

MAD ON THE MOON!

The Moon is Earth's largest natural satellite. It takes 27 days to orbit Earth once and has a cycle of phases from "new" to "full" and "new" again, due to the angle at which we see it lit up by the Sun.

| NEW MOON | WAXING CRESCENT | FIRST QUARTER |

| WAXING GIBBOUS | FULL MOON | WANING GIBBOUS |

| LAST QUARTER | WANING CRESCENT | NEW MOON |

You can demonstrate the phases by shining a flashlight onto an orange from different angles.

| LAST QUARTER | FULL | NEW | WANING CRESCENT |

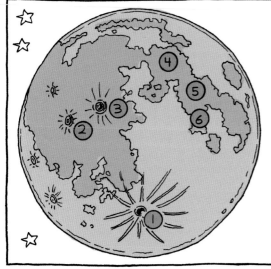

You can see lots of features on the Moon with the naked eye, though binoculars help. Here are six to spot:

CRATERS caused by things hitting the surface; often named after astronomers.
1 Tycho, 2 Kepler, 3 Copernicus

LUNAR SEAS (mares) dark areas of old volcanic activity.
4 Sea of Serenity
5 Sea of Tranquility
6 Apollo 11 landing site

CAROLINE HERSCHEL
"COMET-HUNTER"

BORN:
1750, Germany
DIED:
1848, Germany

Hello! I'm the tiny* German-British astronomer Caroline Herschel —and I'm 97!

Let me fly!

97 TODAY

MARCH 1847

*Caroline stood just 4 feet, 3 inches (1.3 m) tall!

But that's not my only amazing achievement... Oops!

97 TODAY

Free at last!

My big brother, William, was an astronomer for King George III.

WILLIAM HERSCHEL

URANUS

William discovered the planet Uranus in 1781.

In 1782, William made me a telescope so I could help him "sweep the skies."

YOUNGER CAROLINE

I was so good at it that I went on to find eight new comets!

One is named after me!

All of which I recorded and drew in my notebooks.

STAR = +
COMET = ⁓

The king also helped us build what was then the world's largest telescope...

(FROM AN OLD PRINT)

...and he paid me fifty pounds a year to help run it!

£50

I was the first woman to get a salary as a scientist!

£50

In my lifetime, I helped discover over 2,000 stars with William, and won many honors.

But then I did have a very long life!

I'm back!

97 TODAY

Caroline was a comet-hunting hero! Now find out more about these speedy space-travelers!

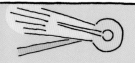 

 Comets are rather odd objects. They are actually frozen lumps of ice and dust and have been nicknamed "dirty snowballs!"

 Though some come close to Earth, comets travel on huge elliptical orbits across the solar system and back around the Sun.

 A comet's tail is a plume of dust and ions (charged particles) that flares out behind it as it gets closer to the Sun.

 Radiation from the Sun hitting the comet means the tail always points directly away from the Sun itself.

 Follow these simple steps to make your own model paper comet, complete with turning tail!

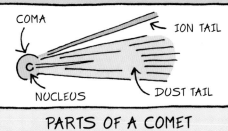

PARTS OF A COMET

A TYPICAL COMET ORBIT

You will need: SHEET OF PAPER, PENCIL, BIT OF TAPE

1 Lay the pencil halfway across the paper and fold the sheet in half.

2 Loosely roll the paper around the pencil a few times.

3 Fix it in place with tape and draw a comet on both sides of your flag.

4 Blow hard at your comet—the tail always turns away from you.

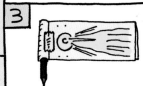 

HOT STUFF!

★ As well as discovering comets and stars with his sister, Caroline, William Herschel also discovered a new type of invisible energy within sunlight that made things hot.

★ Today we call this energy infrared radiation or "IR" for short.

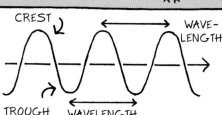

CREST
WAVE-LENGTH
TROUGH WAVELENGTH

Infrared radiation, like visible light, travels as a wave at the speed of light. The distance between two crests or two troughs is a "wavelength."

| RADIO WAVES | MICRO WAVES | INFRARED | VISIBLE LIGHT | ULTRAVIOLET | X-RAYS | GAMMA RAYS |

LESS ENERGY

MORE ENERGY

★ Infrared is part of a range of waves of energy known as the electromagnetic spectrum. Some of this radiation is helpful, but some can be very harmful.

FEEL THE HEAT

All warm objects—including humans—emit infrared. The warmth we feel from a radiator or fire is actually sensors in our skin detecting infrared radiation!

TAKE CONTROL

TV remote controls emit bursts of infrared to tell your set what to do. Like all radiation, IR travels in straight lines and you can reflect it off walls and onto your set.

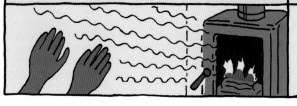

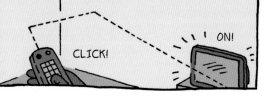

CLICK!   ON!

MATH

Learn about numbers and how they work.

KATHERINE JOHNSON
"HUMAN COMPUTER"

BORN:
1918, USA
DIED:
2020, USA

Hello! I'm African American math legend Katherine Johnson—and I lived to be 101 years old!

Congratulations! You beat me!

Er, thanks...

Who was that?

See page 78!

Anyway, as a child I was mad about math.

YOUNG KATHERINE

One, two, three...

Katherine counted everything—including plates!

At school, I got moved up several years because I was so smart.

Awkward!

And at college, they had to invent new math lessons just for me!

It's some tough stuff!

Great!

TEENAGE KATHERINE

As an adult, I worked for the space agency NASA* as a "human computer!"

HUMAN
NON-HUMAN

*National Aeronautics and Space Administration

And in 1969, I helped create the flight plans for the first Moon landing.

orbit
descent
undocking
landing
separation
Earth

From a NASA report.

Lots of astronauts were grateful to me for my clever calculations—including the Apollo 11 crew.

See page 76.

May I be the first to thank you, Ms. Johnson?

Neil, you did it again!

Sorry, Buzz.

Lots of astronauts all counted on Katherine.
Now you can try counting on yourself!

HANDY MATH

✓ Most people need an occasional hand with their math. Besides counting on your fingers, why not try these "handy" math tricks?

NINE IN A ROW

☆ This gives you the nine times table up to ninety!

1 Lay your hands out flat on a table in front of you and imagine your digits are numbered from 1 to 10.

2 To find the answer for 3 x 9, for example, fold under digit number three.

Now comes a bit of "math magic!"

3 The number of fingers to the left of any folded finger gives you the number of "tens" in the answer. The fingers to the right give you the "units." The answer here: (10 x 2) + 7 = 27!

2 fingers   7 fingers

Try some more "nine times" sums.

TOP TIPS

☆ This is known as Russian peasant multiplication.

1 Imagine your digits are numbered like this (write it on if it helps).

2 Now, to multiply, say 8 x 9, touch together those fingertips.

3 Count all these fingers for the "tens."

7x10=70

2x1=2

Multiply these fingers for the "units."

For any sum, the "tens" are given by counting the two touching fingers and those above them. Here it is "7." The "units" are given by multiplying the lower fingers.

(7x10)+(2x1)=72   Correct!

Try other combinations!

ADA LOVELACE
'THE COMPUTING COUNTESS'

BORN:
1815, England
DIED:
1852, England

Hello! My name is Ada, and I was a real English countess, as well as mad keen on maths!

I was a computing pioneer, and I'm going to show you how to use the next page to read minds!

BASE 10	BASE 2
1	1
2	10
3	11
4	100

Like modern computers, this trick uses Base 2 (binary) rather than the Base 10 we count in.

A fun thing to do with Base 2 is 'reading minds'. Get a friend to pick a number from 1 to 60.

Next, ask them to point only to those shapes on the next page that contain their number.

For every one they point to, secretly add up the first numbers in each shape.

Don't tell me it!

Err...

Don't miss any!

Make them check!

o   1 + 4 +...

These numbers will be 1, 2, 4, 8, 16 and 32 only.

Now pretend to concentrate as if you are reading their mind.

It's coming to me...

Then announce the total you have secretly added up in your head. They will be amazed (hopefully).

Your number was 37!

Wow!

It always works – unless they have missed a shape or you added up wrongly. Try it! You'll look like a math-magician!

Hide this page under a sheet of paper and start 'reading minds' with maths!

MATH MAGIC!

01
03 05 07
09 11 13 15 17
19 21 23 25 27
29 31 33 35 37
39 41 43 45 47
49 51 53 55 57
59

02
03 06 07 10
11 14 15 18 19 22 23
26 27 30 31 34 35 38
39 42 43 45 47 50 51
54 55 58 59

04
05 06
07 12 13
14 15 20 21
22 23 28 29 30
31 36 37 38 39
44 45 46 47 52
53 54 55 60

08 09 10 11 12
13 14 15 24 25
26 27 28 29 30
31 40 41 42 43
44 45 46 47 56
57 58 59 60

16
17 18 19 20
21 22 23 24 25
26 27 28 29 30 31
48 49 50 51 52
53 54 55 56
57 58 59 60

32
33 34 35
36 37 38 39 40
41 42 43 44 45
46 47 48 49 50
51 52 53 54 55
56 57 58 59
60

85

ON A ROLL

Here's some hands-on math that could make you a world record holder one day!

Many people believe it is impossible to fold a piece of paper repeatedly in half more than seven times. But, is that really true? Well, here's one way to find out!

1  Begin with a big sheet of thin paper, such as a sheet of newspaper. The thinner and bigger the better!

2 On a flat surface, fold the paper in half.

Crease the fold, then fold it in half again.

3 Your paper doubles in thickness each time you fold it over. Can you manage seven folds?

START	1 FOLD	2 FOLDS	3 FOLDS
	(1×2)	(2×2)	$(2 \times 2 \times 2)$
1 SHEET THICK	2 SHEETS THICK	4 SHEETS THICK	8 SHEETS THICK

4 FOLDS	5 FOLDS	6 FOLDS	7 FOLDS
$(2 \times 2 \times 2 \times 2)$	$(2 \times 2 \times 2 \times 2 \times 2)$	$(2 \times 2 \times 2 \times 2 \times 2 \times 2)$	$(2 \times 2 \times 2 \times 2 \times 2 \times 2 \times 2)$
Not easy!	Getting harder!	Difficult!	Can you do it?
16 SHEETS THICK	32 SHEETS THICK	64 SHEETS THICK	128 SHEETS THICK

?
Did you get beyond seven folds? If so, well done! But how many sheets thick is a wad of paper folded eight times?

(ANSWER BELOW)

☆ Amazingly, in 2002, an American high school student named Britney Gallivan folded a long, thin strip of paper in half TWELVE times—setting a new world record!

Britney Gallivan (b. 1985) and her toilet paper.

☆ Britney set her record using a roll of very thin toilet paper that was ¾ mile (1.2 km) in length! This is about 60 times longer than a standard toilet paper roll at home (about 66 feet (20 m))!

Why not ask a grown-up for a spare toilet paper roll, find a big open space, and see if you can beat your own personal record?

Math whiz Britney also came up with a clever formula for calculating how thick paper can get when you keep folding it. Just 23 folds gives you a wad over 0.6 mile (1.2 km) thick!

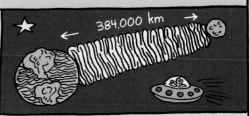

384,000 km

And with just 42 folds you could reach the Moon!

8 folds makes a thickness of 258 sheets (2 × 128)

STANDBY FOR STEM

Science, Technology, Engineering,
and Math—which is your favorite?

MARY SOMERVILLE
"QUEEN OF SCIENCE"

BORN:
1780, Scotland
DIED:
1872, Italy

Mary Somerville was the daughter of a stern admiral in the British Navy.

I have my eye on you, young lady.

Bah!

As a child, Mary loved reading about science and nature.

I'd love to study them!

Bah!

But Mary was forced to learn needlework instead.

What a stitch-up. Bah!

Ha!

DAD →

When she grew up, Mary bought a whole library of books and taught herself math and science!

↙ ADULT MARY

I needed good math just to count them all!

Mary was a natural at advanced math—as well as biology, physics, chemistry, and geology. She became known as the "Queen of science!"

We are not amused. We are delighted!

She was also a clever astronomer.

What a star!

What a star!

Mary predicted the existence of the planet Neptune.

She wrote several best-selling science books, winning her prizes and praise.

Unlike my needlework!

ASTRONOMY
GEOGRAPHY
PHYSICS

"SOMERVILLE CRATER"

Today Mary even has her own crater on the Moon.

Not bad going... for a girl!

Naah!

Mary was a "polymath": a person good at lots of things. Now see what sort of scientist you might be! ⇨

PICTURE YOURSELF

 Mary Somerville explored many areas of science and math. Today we call these "STEM" subjects: Science, Technology, Engineering, and Math.

✓ This fun test shows a series of science careers. Pick a subject, then follow your favorite path to a possible future STEM career!

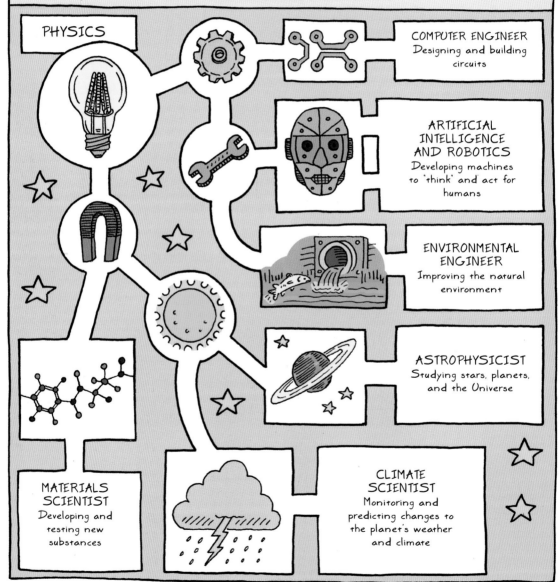

PHYSICS

COMPUTER ENGINEER
Designing and building circuits

ARTIFICIAL INTELLIGENCE AND ROBOTICS
Developing machines to "think" and act for humans

ENVIRONMENTAL ENGINEER
Improving the natural environment

ASTROPHYSICIST
Studying stars, planets, and the Universe

MATERIALS SCIENTIST
Developing and testing new substances

CLIMATE SCIENTIST
Monitoring and predicting changes to the planet's weather and climate

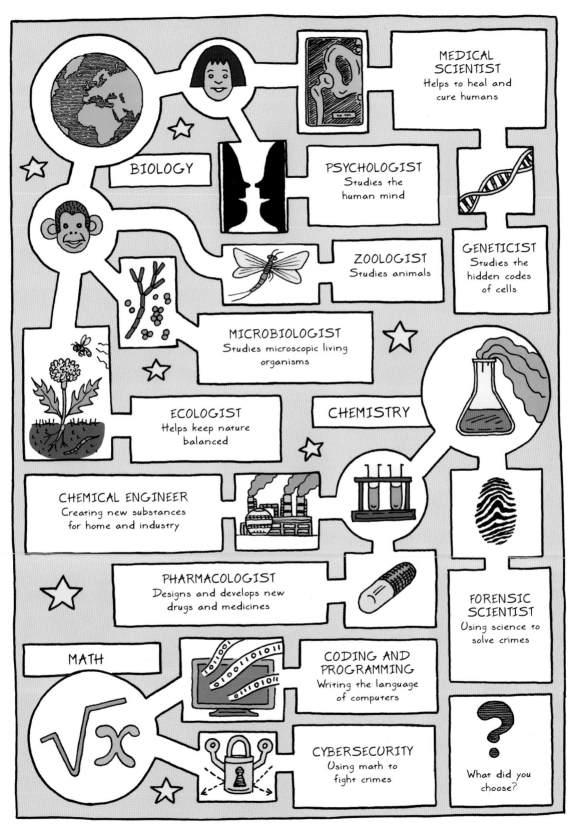

MEDICAL SCIENTIST
Helps to heal and cure humans

BIOLOGY

PSYCHOLOGIST
Studies the human mind

GENETICIST
Studies the hidden codes of cells

ZOOLOGIST
Studies animals

MICROBIOLOGIST
Studies microscopic living organisms

ECOLOGIST
Helps keep nature balanced

CHEMISTRY

CHEMICAL ENGINEER
Creating new substances for home and industry

PHARMACOLOGIST
Designs and develops new drugs and medicines

FORENSIC SCIENTIST
Using science to solve crimes

MATH

CODING AND PROGRAMMING
Writing the language of computers

CYBERSECURITY
Using math to fight crimes

What did you choose?

MIKE BARFIELD
"SCIENTIFIC SCRIBBLER"

BORN:
1962, Leicester,
England

Hello! My name is Mike, and I wrote and drew this book!

It's been great fun as this book is a combination of two of my favorite things...

...comics!

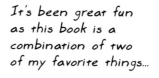

... and fun science!

There's a better model on page 40!

← ME

← "HAMMY"

This is me at home when I was about five years old.

I can still remember my first ever day at school at around the same age. Another child showed me how to make a simple paper plane to cheer me up.

← VERY BASIC PAPER DART!

See page 31

I'm still making them over fifty years later.

...and they still cheer me up!

However, what really got me excited was a fellow pupil who demonstrated some simple science magic.

They pushed a handkerchief in a glass into a tank of water and it stayed dry!

Find out why on page 44!

From that moment, I was hooked on science for life!

Over the next years, I copied all the experiments in junior science books we had at home.

GROWING A BEAN SEED

NEWTON COLOR WHEEL

STATIC ELECTRICITY

Just like those in this book!

By the age of twelve, I was crazy about wildlife, especially birds.

I drew them all the time!

One of my actual drawings.

Eventually I went and spent three years at university studying biology, but – remember all those comics? – I also wanted to write and draw jokes.

So, that's what I do nowadays! I make funny science books for children – best of both worlds!

And it's all thanks to copying these people from the past!

BYE!

Thanks for reading "Copycat Science." Now get experimenting yourself!

ATOM
A building block of matter. Atoms are very small and fit together with other atoms to make everything in the Universe. They have a central nucleus containing particles called protons and neutrons, surrounded by electrons.

BLACK HOLE
An area of space where super-dense matter has such a strong gravitational pull that nothing can escape from it—not even light.

CELL
The smallest functioning unit of a living thing. Cells come in many different types according to what job they do. Plant cells have rigid walls to support them.

ELECTROMAGNET
A coil of wire wound around a central iron core. When an electric current flows through the coil, it produces a magnetic effect.

EVOLUTION
The natural process by which new species arise from earlier ones by changes over time.

GERMINATION
The start of growth of a new plant from a seed or a spore.

GLAND
An organ in an animal that produces and secretes substances for use in the body.

LARVA
A young form of an animal such as an insect, often looking quite different than the adult. For example, caterpillars are the larvae (plural) of butterflies and moths.

LIFECYCLE
The stages a living thing may pass through before it reproduces and dies. For example, an adult silk moth starts as an egg, before becoming a caterpillar, then spinning a cocoon from which it finally emerges.

MOLECULE
A group of atoms bonded together. The atoms can be identical, such as the oxygen molecules in air (O_2), or different, forming a chemical compound.

NATIVE
A word used for living things that are normally found in a certain ecosystem. For example, a lion is native to the African savanna, but a polar bear is not.

NUTRIENTS
The substances that living things need to survive, grow, and reproduce. They include not just food, but also minerals and vitamins.

ORBIT
The regular curved path that a planet, moon, comet, or manmade satellite takes around another body such as the Sun.

ORGANISM
A living thing. On Earth, organisms range in size from microscopic single-celled lifeforms such as bacteria, to giant multi-celled animals such as the blue whale.

PIONEERING
The first person to attempt or achieve something new is said to be a pioneer.

POLLUTANTS
Substances introduced into an environment or ecosystem that have a harmful effect. Many pollutants are manmade.

PROPULSION
The act of pushing or driving an object forward. It requires a force acting in the opposite direction.

RADIATION
Energy emitted in the form of electromagnetic waves—such as radio waves, visible light, or infrared.

REPRODUCE
When living things make copies of themselves to ensure the survival of their species over time.

SATELLITE (NATURAL)
An orbiting object such as Earth's moon. Earth is also orbited by many artificial (manmade) satellites such as the International Space Station.

SPECIMEN
An individual organism collected for scientific study.

VOLUME
The amount of space that a substance or object takes up. Scientists measure it in cubic feet (ft^3) or cubic meters (m^3).

INDEX

PICTURE CREDITS

center (c), bottom (b), top (t), left (l), right (r)

10cr N. Grew, The anatomy of plants: Wellcome Collection. Attribution 4.0 International (CC BY 4.0); 24cl Raymond Gosling/King's College London; 42cr Library of Congress Prints and Photographs Division; 62 Reproduction of drawings illustrating British Patent No. 347,206, filed 16th January 1930; 64lc Copy of the Kitab al-Manazir (MS Fatih 3212, vol. 1, fol. 81b, Süleimaniye Mosque Library, Istanbul); 68bc Wellcome Collection gallery (2018-04-03): https://wellcomecollection.org/works/r8h48ctw; 74c http://moro.imss.fi.it/lettura/LetturaWEB.DLL?AZIONE=IMG&TESTO=E__Y&PARAM=03-66j; 76tr National Aeronautics and Space Administration; 76tl NASA; 78bl Leisure Hour, Nov 2,1867, page 729; 82 NASA